PRIMARY SOURCES OF
FAMOUS PEOPLE IN AMERICAN HISTORY™

# GEORGE ARMSTRONG CUSTER

## GENERAL OF THE U.S. CAVALRY
## GENERAL DE LA CABALLERÍA ESTADOUNIDENSE

THEODORE LINK

TRADUCCIÓN AL ESPAÑOL:
TOMÁS GONZÁLEZ

rosen central
Primary Source™
Editorial Buenas Letras™

The Rosen Publishing Group, Inc., New York

Published in 2004 by The Rosen Publishing Group, Inc.
29 East 21st Street, New York, NY 10010

**First Bilingual Edition 2004**
First English Edition 2004

## Cataloging Data

Link, Theodore.
[George Armstrong Custer. Bilingual]
George Armstrong Custer / by Theodore Link.— 1st ed.
    v. cm. — (Grandes personajes en la historia de los Estados Unidos)
Summary: A biography of the Civil War general known for his part in the disastrous battle at the Little Bighorn in 1876.
Includes bibliographical references (p.  ) and index.
Contents: Autie—The Civil War—Going West—Chief Sitting Bull and Little Bighorn—Custer's last stand.
ISBN 0-8239-4158-2 (lib. bdg.)
1. Custer, George Armstrong, 1839–1876—Juvenile literature. 2. Generals—United States—Biography—Juvenile literature. 3. United States. Army—Biography—Juvenile literature. 4. United States—History—Civil War, 1861–1865—Biography—Juvenile literature. 5. Indians of North America—Wars—Great Plains—Juvenile literature. 6. Little Bighorn, Battle of the, Mont., 1876—Juvenile literature. 7. Little Bighorn, Battle of the, Mont., 1876. [1. Custer, George Armstrong, 1839–1876. 2. Generals. 3. Spanish language materials—Bilingual.]
I. Title. II. Series: Primary sources of famous people in American history.
E467.1.C99L56 2003
973.8'2'092—dc21

*Manufactured in the United States of America*

**Photo credits:** cover National Archives and Records Administration; pp. 5, 7 National Portrait Gallery, Smithsonian Institute/Art Resource, NY; p. 9 Library of Congress Prints and Photographs Division; p. 11 © Medford Historical Society Collection/ Corbis; p.13 © Bettmann/Corbis; pp. 15 (X-33621), 21 (X-31704), 29 (top) (X-31275) Denver Public Library, Western History Collection; p. 17 © Corbis; p. 19 © Hulton/Archive/Getty Images; pp. 23, 25 Western History Collection, University of Oklahoma; pp. 27, 29 (bottom) © North Wind Picture Archives.

# CONTENTS

# CONTENIDO

# 1 AUTIE

In his short life, George Armstrong Custer became a famous leader. He became a legend after his stunning death at the Little Bighorn.

He was born on December 5, 1839, in New Rumley, Ohio. His family called him "Armstrong." He could not say his name. He called himself "Autie." The name stuck.

---

# 1 AUTIE

En su corta vida, George Armstrong Custer llegó a ser un famoso jefe militar. Se convirtió en leyenda después de su pasmosa muerte en la batalla de *Little Bighorn.*

Custer nació el 5 de diciembre de 1839, en New Rumley, Ohio. Sus padres le pusieron "Armstrong". De niño no podía pronunciar su nombre y se llamaba a sí mismo "Autie". Y ese nombre se le quedó.

**George "Autie" Custer as a cadet at West Point around 1860**

George "Autie" Custer como cadete en West Point, en 1860 aproximadamente

Autie and his father loved jokes. No one in the family was safe from their pranks.

Autie went to West Point to become a soldier. He had trouble following rules. He made his friends laugh at the wrong times. Autie got into a lot of trouble. But his classmates made him a leader.

---

A Autie y a su padre les encantaba hacer chistes. Nadie en la familia estaba a salvo de sus bromas.

Autie ingresó a West Point para convertirse en soldado, pero encontraba difícil seguir las reglas. Hacía reír a sus compañeros en momentos inoportunos. Autie se metía en muchos problemas, pero sus compañeros de clase lo consideraban un líder.

**George Armstrong Custer as a brigadier general in 1863**

George Armstrong Custer como brigadier general en 1863

# 2 THE CIVIL WAR

"Autie" Custer graduated from West Point in 1861. The Civil War had begun. The South had broken away from the United States.

Custer wanted to help the country stay whole. He joined the cavalry, gathering news about the enemy. Very good at his job, he quickly moved up in rank. In 1863, Custer became the youngest general in the army!

---

# 2 LA GUERRA CIVIL

"Autie" Custer se graduó en West Point en 1861. La Guerra Civil había comenzado. El Sur se había separado de Estados Unidos.

Custer deseaba que el país permaneciera unido. Ingresó en la caballería y su misión consistía en obtener información sobre el enemigo. Era muy bueno en su trabajo y ascendió de rango rápidamente. En 1863, Custer se convirtió en el general más joven del ejército.

HARPER'S WEEKLY.

A JOURNAL OF CIVILIZATION.

VOL. VIII.—No. 377.] NEW YORK, SATURDAY, MARCH 19, 1864. [$4.00 FOR FOUR MONTHS.
$3.00 PER YEAR IN ADVANCE.

Entered according to Act of Congress, in the Year 1864, by Harper & Brothers, in the Clerk's Office of the District Court for the Southern District of New York.

Custer pictured on the cover of *Harper's Weekly* in 1864.

Custer aparece en la portada de *Harper's Weekly* en 1864.

His job was to lead a Michigan cavalry group. The soldiers were very loyal to him. Custer had his own personal flag. It helped his men find him in battle. He became one of the best leaders of either side.

By the war's end in 1865, Custer was famous. He had helped the North beat the South. To people in the North, he was a hero.

---

Su trabajo consistía en dirigir un grupo de caballería de Michigan. Los soldados le tenían mucha lealtad. Custer tenía su bandera personal, que permitía a sus soldados localizarlo en las batallas. Se convirtió en uno de los mejores jefes militares de los dos bandos de la guerra.

Cuando terminó la guerra en 1865, Custer era famoso. Había ayudado a que el Norte derrotara al Sur. Era un héroe para la gente del Norte.

This portrait of Custer and his wife, Libbie, was taken between 1860 and 1864.

Retrato de Custer y su esposa Libbie tomado entre 1860 y 1864.

# 3  GOING WEST

After the war, Custer became a lieutenant colonel in the Seventh Cavalry. The cavalry's job was to help keep peace in the South.

The army sent the Seventh Cavalry to the West in 1867. People were settling there. The American government encouraged people to live in the West.

---

# 3  CON DESTINO AL OESTE

Después de la guerra, Custer fue nombrado teniente coronel de la Séptima Caballería. La misión de la caballería era mantener la paz en el Sur.

En 1867, el ejército envió a la Séptima Caballería al Oeste. La gente estaba colonizando aquella región. El gobierno estadounidense animaba a la gente a que se fuera a vivir al Oeste.

**Custer photographed with his Indian scouts and dogs**

Custer fotografiado con sus perros y con guías indios

13

But the Indians had lived there for a long time. The tribes were angry. Some declared war on the settlers. Custer's cavalry worked to protect the settlers.

In 1868, Custer led his men against the Cheyenne Indians. Custer's men beat them at the Washita River. Most of the tribe gave up. Custer was a hero again.

---

Pero los indios habían vivido en el Oeste desde hacía muchísimo tiempo. Las tribus estaban enojadas y algunas les declararon la guerra a los colonos. La caballería de Custer protegía a los colonos.

En 1868, Custer dirigió a sus hombres contra los indios cheyenes. Los hombres de Custer los derrotaron en el río Washita. La mayoría de los miembros de la tribu se dio por vencida. Custer otra vez se convirtió en héroe.

THE PLATTE RIVER AT NORTH PLATTE.—Sketched by T. R. Davis.—[See First Page.]

### ETHAN ALLEN.

We give on page 485 a handsome engraving of the fast trotter, Ethan Allen. The original of this picture was taken by instantaneous photography by Rockwood, and is as perfect a picture of the animal as can be obtained.

Prominent as Ethan Allen is in the Racing Calendar, it is almost impossible to give the truth in regard to his pedigree and performances. He is now a little over 18 years of age, having been foaled in Hague, Warren County, New York, on June 19, 1849. He was bred by Mr. O. S. Roe, who formerly owned him, and from whom we have obtained the few reliable statements which are to be had regarding his pedigree. His sire was Vermont Black Hawk, and his dam a gray mare whose pedigree is unknown, and who was brought to New York a short time before the birth of Ethan Allen. He is supposed to be a descendant on the mother's side of Messenger, but this is not positively known, although it is frequently very positively stated.

Of his performances previous to the fast race made by him on June 21, 1867, we know little that is positive. He was beaten by Flora Temple at Baltimore, December 1, 1859, in 2.25½; again at Fashion Course during the same season in 2.25; and beat Columbus, Jun., at the National Horse Fair, Boston, in 1859, in 2.31.

His most remarkable trot was made on Fashion Course, Long Island, on June 21, 1 where he and his running mate beat the fa Dexter in harness in the remarkable time 2.15, 2.16, and 2.19. The horses were in sp did condition at the time, and the day and t were particularly fine, but no one expected any thing like the extraordinary speed displa by both animals would be exhibited. The t has never been beaten in this country.

TRAVELING ON A PRAIRIE CANON.—[See First Page.]

GENERAL CUSTER'S INTERVIEW WITH PAWNEE KILLER.—[See First Page.]

**Four drawings from *Harper's Weekly* portray Custer with Sioux Indians.**

Cuatro dibujos de *Harper's Weekly* muestran a Custer con indios sioux.

Custer was a great hunter. Many people wanted to hunt with him. Custer once took a Russian duke with him when he went hunting! They became good friends.

———◆◆◆———

Custer fue un gran cazador. Muchos querían salir de cacería con él. Custer una vez llevó a un duque ruso a una de sus cacerías y se hicieron buenos amigos.

General Custer and others pose with a grizzly bear they killed on a hunt in 1874.

El general Custer y otros posan con un oso gris que mataron en una cacería en 1874.

## 4 CHIEF SITTING BULL AND THE LITTLE BIGHORN

In 1873, Custer led his men into the Dakota Territory. They blazed a trail through the wilderness. The Northern Pacific Railroad laid its tracks along this path. Custer enjoyed the trip. He got to show off as a hunter and a woodsman.

---

## 4 TORO SENTADO Y LA BATALLA DE LITTLE BIGHORN

En 1873, Custer llevó a sus hombres a Dakota. Abrieron un camino a través de una región agreste. La compañía de trenes *Northern Pacific* tendió sus rieles a lo largo de ese camino. Custer disfrutó de esta misión, pues le permitió exhibir sus habilidades como cazador y hombre del bosque.

When the railroads reached across the West, it became easier for white people to settle on Indian lands.

Cuando los ferrocarriles cruzaron el Oeste, a la gente blanca se le hizo más fácil establecerse en las tierras de los indios.

19

In 1874, miners found gold in the Dakota Territory. Many people moved there to get rich.

The Sioux Indians owned the land. They did not want settlers to take it. They declared war. Chief Sitting Bull brought many of the Sioux tribes together for the fight.

———◆◆◆———

En 1874, los mineros encontraron oro en Dakota. Muchos viajaron allí para hacerse ricos.

Los indios sioux eran los dueños de esas tierras. No querían que los colonos se las quitaran y declararon la guerra. El jefe indio Toro Sentado unió a muchas de las tribus sioux para la lucha.

**Custer led a large expedition across the plains in 1874.**

Custer dirigió una gran expedición que cruzó las praderas en 1874.

By 1876, the United States wanted to force Indians onto reservations. Custer was ordered to drive the tribes off of their land. Custer had to find Sitting Bull and his warriors.

The Sioux were gathered near the Little Bighorn River. The Seventh Cavalry got ready for battle.

---

Hacia 1876, Estados Unidos trató de obligar a los indios a vivir en reservaciones. A Custer se le ordenó sacar a los indios de sus tierras. Custer tenía que buscar a Toro Sentado y sus guerreros.

Los sioux se habían reunido cerca del río *Little Bighorn*. La Séptima Caballería se dispuso a enfrentarlos en una batalla.

Sitting Bull is shown here on Indian land in the Dakota Territory.

Toro Sentado aparece aquí en el territorio de los sioux de Dakota.

23

# 5 CUSTER'S LAST STAND

Custer attacked the Indians on June 25, 1876. He and 210 horsemen charged through a pass at the Little Bighorn. Another group of his men attacked the Indian camp from the side. Other soldiers circled around to do the same.

Sitting Bull's men drove away the first group. Custer and his soldiers reached the battlefield too late to help them.

---

# 5 EL ÚLTIMO COMBATE

Custer atacó a los indios el 25 de junio de 1876. Él y 210 jinetes se lanzaron a la carga en un paso del río *Little Bighorn*. Otro grupo de sus hombres atacó un costado del campamento indio. Otros soldados se movían en círculos haciendo lo mismo.

Los hombres de Toro Sentado rechazaron el primer grupo enemigo. Custer y sus soldados llegaron muy tarde a ayudarles.

Sitting Bull refused to sign a land treaty with the American government. As a result, white people were afraid of him.

Toro Sentado rehusó firmar un tratado de tierras con el gobierno estadounidense. Por esa razón los blancos le temían.

News of the battle spread. Many people were shocked by Custer's death. Many people mourned.

Custer was only thirty-five years old when he died. He was a famous leader. People wonder what he might have done if he had lived longer.

---

La noticia de la batalla se difundió con rapidez. Muchos estaban consternados por la muerte de Custer. Muchos estuvieron de luto.

Cuando murió, Custer tenía sólo treinta y cinco años de edad. Fue un famoso jefe militar. La gente se pregunta lo que hubiese logrado de haber vivido más tiempo.

Above: Grave markers on the site of the Battle of the Little Bighorn.
Below: Here are the gravestones of Custer and his men as they look today.

Arriba: Tumbas en el sitio de la batalla de *Little Bighorn*. Abajo: Lápidas de Custer y sus hombres, tal como se encuentran en la actualidad.

# TIMELINE

December 5, 1839—George Armstrong "Autie" Custer is born.

1863—Custer becomes a general in the Union army.

June 25, 1876—Custer and 210 of his men die at the Battle of the Little Bighorn.

1861—Custer graduates from West Point and joins the cavalry to fight for the Union army during the Civil War.

1873—Custer and the Seventh Cavalry go to the Dakota Territory to blaze a trail for the Northern Pacific Railroad.

# CRONOLOGÍA

5 de diciembre de 1839—Nace George Armstrong "Autie" Custer.

1863—Custer se convierte en general del ejército de la Unión.

25 de junio de 1876—Custer y 210 de sus hombres mueren en la batalla de *Little Bighorn*.

1861—Custer se gradúa en West Point e ingresa en la caballería para luchar por el ejército de la Unión durante la Guerra Civil.

1873—Custer y la Séptima Caballería van a Dakota con la misión de abrir un camino para la compañía de trenes *Northern Pacific Railroad*.

# GLOSSARY

**cavalry (KA-vul-ree)** A group of soldiers who ride horses into battle.

**general (JEN-rul)** The person in charge of leading; the army's highest rank.

**lieutenant colonel (loo-TEH-nent KER-nul)** The rank in the army just below a full colonel.

**officer (AH-fih-sur)** A leader in the army.

**rank (RANK)** A soldier's level of authority in the army. For example, a general is a high rank.

**regiment (REH-jih-ment)** A group in the military; a large group of soldiers led by a colonel.

**West Point (WEST POYNT)** A United States military academy.

## WEB SITES

Due to the changing nature of Internet links, the Rosen Publishing Group, Inc., has developed an online list of Web sites related to the subject of this book. This site is updated regularly. Please use this link to access the list:

http://www.rosenlinks.com/fpah/gacu

## GLOSARIO

**caballería (la)** Grupo de soldados que combaten a caballo en las batallas.

**general (el)** Persona encargada de mandar; es el rango más alto del ejército.

**oficial (el, la)** Persona con funciones de jefe en el ejército.

**rango (el)** Grado de autoridad de los soldados en el ejército. El de general, por ejemplo, es un rango alto.

**regimiento (el)** Grupo grande de soldados, dirigidos por un coronel.

**teniente coronel (el, la)** Rango del ejército que está inmediatamente antes que el de coronel.

**West Point** Academia militar estadounidense.

## SITIOS WEB

Debido a las constantes modificaciones en los sitios de Internet, Rosen Publishing Group, Inc., ha desarrollado un listado de sitios Web relacionados con el tema de este libro. Este sitio se actualiza con regularidad. Por favor, usa este enlace para acceder a la lista:

http://www.rosenlinks.com/fpah/gacu

# INDEX

## ABOUT THE AUTHOR

Theodore Link is an author living in Chicago.

## ÍNDICE

## ACERCA DEL AUTOR

Theodore Link es escritor. Vive en Chicago.